MW00962269

Find What You Were Born For

Discover Your Inborn Skills,

Forge Your Own Path,

Live The Life You Want

Maximize Your Self-Confidence

By Zoe McKey

Communication Coach and Social Development

Trainer

zoemckey@gmail.com

www.zoemckey.com

Thank you for choosing my book! I would like to show my appreciation for the trust you gave me by giving a **FREE GIFT** for you! Get it following the link below:

www.zoemckey.com

The checklist talks about *5 key elements of building self-confidence* and contains extra actionable worksheets with practice exercises for deeper learning.

Learn how to:

- Solve 80% of you self-esteem issues with one simple change
- Keep your confidence permanent without falling back to self-doubt
- Not fall into the trap of promising words
- Overcome anxiety
- Be confident among other people

Table of Contents

Introduction

Two years ago I met a man who, in the literal sense of the word, was very successful. He was a recognized expert in his industry, rich, and deeply, utterly unhappy. Back then I was working fourteen hours a day from Monday through Saturday and I was irritated by his bad attitude.

- *Poor rich guy, what does he know about struggle? He doesn't know what to do with his own good fortune...*

But after my bitterness disappeared, I had some other interesting thoughts. *I hate my job, but I struggle for money in the hope that it will make me happy. This guy clearly has money but not happiness. He hates his job just like me, and he suffers just like me. There must be something else out there. What is the key to happiness? Since it isn't money or success.*

What is it?

After some thought, I concluded that a Richie Rich's problem was that he hated his work. He didn't find any value in it. I knew he was a passionate cook, but he'd never tried it professionally. I was convinced that if he followed his passion he'd be a happy man.

Not long after that, I met a woman who was a fire dancer. She loved it. When she was dancing her face glowed. When I went to congratulate her after an amazing performance, she told me sadly, "Yes, I love doing it, but I was kicked out of my apartment because I can't pay my bill. I can't make a living from fire dancing, because…" And she proceeded to tell me all the reasons fire dancing was NOT profitable.

I was confused, what's wrong with people? If you earn money doing something you hate, then you're unhappy. If you do something you love, you die of hunger and are also unhappy. What is the solution?

How can a person be successful AND happy? Where is the thin ice that doesn't break if you step on it and walk to a life worth living?

There are three factors a person should possess in order to achieve success and happiness:

- Passion – for happiness
- Skill – for success
- Usefulness – for money

The ideas in this book changed my life and drove me to write this book and share them with others. The book will show you how to find happiness by answering the three questions above. What is your passion? What are you the best at? How can you earn money doing it?

In my research, I was initially touched by Professor Howard Gardner's multiple intelligence theory. This theory triggered a lot of discussion, but one thing is true: whether we consider these intelligence types to be skills, talents, or literal intelligence types, they influence our lives greatly and are a crucial factor in individual development and happiness.

But I don't want to spoil everything, read this book and find the answers for yourself!

Chapter 1: What is success?

Success means something different to me, to you, and to the other seven billion people living on the Earth. Some of us aim higher; some of us are satisfied with less. Some people seek money; some people seek love or appreciation. Some want it all at once.

If animals have a survival instinct, we can say that humans have a "success instinct." The drive for success pushes us forward, keeps us in motion, helps us create incredible things. We always want more. This is why when we complete a task we are not satisfied for long but instead think of the next step and how we can do *more.*

Have you given any thought to why some people are more successful than others? Why they are happier, richer, and more free.

Those who don't have goals in life are sadder, pessimistic, always depressed, and often angry. Mental and physical illnesses can attack this kind of person more easily.

There is a group between the super-happy, rich and active minority, and the passive majority. There are people who have goals, who even achieve some successes, but are not happy and their lives don't seem to move from point A to point B. These people put a lot of effort into what they do, but hardly ever find the fulfillment they're looking for. This is mostly because of their jobs.

We spend most of our adult lives working on something. We go to our workplace at least five days a week. If we do something we hate, dislike, or simply feel apathetic about, all five days of our week will be stressful, unhappy or, in the best case, mediocre.

Is this success? Is this a life lived to the fullest?

My dear reader, now you must be thinking: *this is not so simple, I can't change now, I'm too old, or what does the author know about me?*

As someone who had to "borrow" food from her dorm's common fridge to survive, who had to wash blood vessels in a butchery, who worked as a car tire loader in a factory, but eventually became a translator and then a full-time writer and social development coach, I can honestly say it is possible to change. With little money in my account, I made a risky decision, but I knew what I wanted. Thanks to the bad jobs, I knew what I didn't want to do long term. So I changed my life – and I tell you I've never been happier or lived better.

Yesterday (Sunday), I had a conversation with an old friend. She asked what I was doing. I answered that I was working. She replied, "Oh poor you, that must be so awful to have to work on the weekend." And when I heard that sentence a divine spark hit me. No, on the contrary, it is so awesome! I'm blessed; I am happy; I love to do what I'm doing! Her negative response only helped increase my awareness of my blissful situation. I could have easily chosen to not do anything on Sunday, but I wanted to write this book for you. I was so inspired that I couldn't think of a more enjoyable Sunday activity.

My point is that it matters what you spend your days doing. In the end I got a good job as a decently paid translator. And I was good. People liked my style. I ended up being the personal simultaneous translator for the general manager of a multinational company. I don't mean to brag; I just want to make it clear that I had a good job. But I wasn't happy, and I left it without regret.

The trigger for my personal change was a book called *Frames of Mind: The theory of multiple intelligences* by Howard Gardner. In this book the professor presents his theory of multiple intelligences (verbal, logical, intrapersonal, interpersonal, musical, spatial, kinesthetic, naturalist, and existential). It was the first time I had thought about my strengths? I thought about what I love doing the most, what gives me passion, and what I could easily do long-term (the next sixty years for instance).

Soon another question followed: would the activity I chose bring me success? Did I have enough knowledge to start it?

There has never been an easier time to follow your dreams. Thanks to technology so much information is available to broaden your knowledge in any field. We can develop any skill or intelligence. We live in a world of possibilities.

I am a huge fan of Brian Tracy. I love the guy. One of his sentences inspired me to dig deeper in finding a correlation between the multiple intelligence types and success. This was the sentence:

- "It was proven that there is no correlation between success and intelligence, appearance, literacy and connections. In some cases they are helpful, but no direct connection can be found."

Quite counterintuitive, right? However his sentence sparked a challenge in me to find the strongest connection and closest correlation between success and these intelligence types.

Intelligence is influenced by behavior, thus, with study and practice, thoughts and mindset can be improved. And if we choose the right path to invest in and to develop, the limit of our ability is the starry sky.

What is the right path? Is it something our parents want us to do? Is it something society pushes us to do? Is it something that brings us a lot of money?

Or, is it something that gives us a reason to wake up every day, a reason to go for it, to learn and enjoy work without considering it a burden? Is it something we feel a constant passion for? Does doing it fill us with a deep feeling of contentment and a strong sense of growth? Is it something we feel *we were born to do*?

Are you a passionate cook, but think it is an impossible way to make a living? Ask Gordon Ramsey if he makes a decent living.

Do you wake up and go to sleep with melodies in your head? Could you play the piano before you could write? Did your parents always tell you music was for hobos and you'd never be able to pay your bills from it? Ask Celine Dion if she can pay her bills.

You always dreamed of being a world famous sport star, but people considered your dreams ridiculous. Ask Diego Maradona if his dreams were ridiculous.

If it was possible for them, why isn't it for you? Never let another's defeatist approach bring you down! If you have a calling, go for it! Do it! Believe in yourself!

How do you believe in yourself? By constantly proving those who say you can't do it wrong, AND by constantly proving yourself right by saying, "YES, I CAN DO IT!"

How do you do that? By doing something you are passionate about, something you have a talent for, something that calls you like flowers call the bees. If you have a *day-by-day confirmation* in the form of a small or big success, you will never feel you're heading the wrong way. In small successes you can understand anything. Go for a walk instead of watching TV, drink water instead of coke, throw out the useless stuff from your wardrobe. If any of these actions bring you a closer to your goal then they are immense steps forward.

The point of this book is neither to convince you to resign your highly paid job today, nor to follow a raw, instinctual calling and leave the rest behind.

My aim is to teach you the main areas of intelligence, and personal development. The point of this book is:

- to get you thinking about your strongest innate abilities that you could build to the expert level,
- to give practical advice on how to improve these innate abilities,
- to help you improve the weaker intelligences you'd like to be better at,
- to give you the kick you need to go out of your comfort zone and do something that fills your happiness tank,
- and to educate you on the latest intelligence research.

This book approaches success like no other has before. In reading it you have nothing to lose and everything to gain.

Let's start this journey!

Chapter 2: A brief history of intelligence development

We were, and still are, part of nature. Historically, humans were not on the top of the food chain. They had to fight to stay alive. And these fights weren't simple ones. But the acquisition of food, the race preservation, and the fight to stay alive slowly began to rise from the instinctual level to the conscious level.

When the first anthropoid climbed down from the tree and discovered primitive tools, human civilization started to distinguish itself from other species. And how far were we from iPhones and rocket science?

One Stone Age ancestor threw a rock and acknowledged with interest how fast that rock traveled the distance between him and his prey. He realized that throwing rocks was much better than sticks to hunt a running, jumping, or flying animal.

Our ancestors slowly began to develop different kinds of weapons for attacking, for protection, and for household use. The roots of intelligence awakened in their brains. They figured out that working in team increased the chances of making a successful hunt. More rocks equaled more possibilities. Rudimentary teamwork, right?

They had already begun to study human qualities even back then. Who is the fastest runner? Who is the most accurate rock thrower? Who is the slowest? Who is the one they had to be faster than to not end up in the stomach of a beast?

Our ancestors also found "special" people they shared between their communities. These people could explain unfamiliar natural phenomena (were good in verbal, logical, and interpersonal intelligence) and became tribal shamans. To lead it was essential to have physical power, courage, speed, awareness, and persuasion skills (kinesthetic, logical, verbal, spatial intelligence). A good hunter had to be fast, know how to read tracks, had to throw accurately (physical, logical, spatial intelligence). Some were good in imitating animal sounds (musical intelligence), and I could go on and on with the examples.

Everything can be measured nowadays, even intelligence. The measurement of intelligence started to be taken more seriously in the second half of the 1800s. In the beginning, researchers measured how quickly the subject responded to certain external stimuli. The reaction time, or quick reflexes, were not strongly connected with for example results achieved in school.

Sir Francis Galton was the first person to create a test to measure intellectual abilities. In 1884, he wanted to prove that British scientific greats and normal citizens could be separated into groups based on the size of their heads. The parameters tested were auditory threshold, reaction time, and visual acuity. The test didn't prove to be successful. Based on the criterion above, no significant difference could be made between a genius and a normal citizen.

Researchers dug deeper and developed more comprehensive tests. Based on the answers given they could rank subjects at different levels. With this new system they could decide how many years ahead or behind a child was in his or her subjects. Each person was ranked with above, below, or average qualities. Mental age appeared as a concept. And it was measurable.

Alfred Binet, a French psychologist also thought there was a correlation between the size of the brain and intelligence, however no significant evidence proved it. The size of the human brain is not proportional to intelligence.

The first intelligence test appeared in the beginning of the 20th century and it was called the Binet-Simon scale. In the years that followed, it went through a lot of changes and corrections. The test was adapted to the new understandings revealed in intelligence research. William Stern introduced the intelligence quotient as a concept first in 1912.

Dividing mental age by real age and multiplying by 100 calculate IQ.

The Stanford-Binet test was used in 1916 at Stanford University as the first large-scale, representative sample IQ measurement. Since then professionals have specifically applied it to all areas of life.

It is important to mention another variable, which measures the correlation among different cognitive tasks. Proposed by English psychologist Charles Spearman, this variable is called the *g factor*.

Spearman initially researched a group of elementary school children who performed seemingly unrelated school subjects like math, literature, and music. He discovered that some subjects were in fact positively related. Children who did great on literature tests, tended to do well on math tests also. Some who failed one type of test had a high probability of failing another type as well.

Following this thread, Spearman concluded that mental performance could be conceived as a single universal ability factor, which he called g. This was followed by a large number of smaller, task-specific ability factors.

Today's model looks like a family tree with three levels and g factor at the apex as the variable for all cognitive tasks. A level lower there are eight, more general factors such as fluid intelligence (Gf), crystallized intelligence (Gc), broad visual perception (Gv), and others. The third level consists of a large number of narrow factors.

However, this g factor theory has been questioned by a handful of psychologists. One of them was the gentleman I mentioned in Chapter 1, Howard Gardner, who came up with the multiple intelligence theory. This theory is based on the thesis of uncorrelated abilities.

I will present an overview of the multiple intelligence theory in the next chapters. In fact, I've based my entire book on Gardner's idea. Although he's been criticized over the years, one fact is true. The different areas of intelligence are vital parts of each individual's personal development. I think it is very important for us to recognize the areas in which we excel and those areas we need to improve.

Let's explore the pros and cons in Gardner's theory.

Chapter 3: Multiple intelligence theory

The human brain is complex. I won't go into the details; I'll leave that for super-scientific anatomy books. I will briefly mention the main differences between our right and left hemispheres.

The *right hemisphere* is responsible for speaking (word articulation), desires, rhymes, rhythm, the perception of images, colors, planning, music, and imagination.

The *left hemisphere* interprets words, schedules, numbers, makes logical correlations, processes special vision, boundary line perception, and builds identity.

Why is this important? The two hemispheres are responsible for totally different functions. We can state that the right hemisphere is responsible for creativity and the left hemisphere for more rational functions. It is very rare that a person's two brain hemispheres share functions equally. It's more common for one hemisphere to be more active and dominant.

In other words, you could say that some people have better verbal and some have better logical intelligence. In 1983 however, as professor at Harvard University, Howard Gardner came up with a new theory, the theory of multiple intelligences. He summarized his thoughts in the book, *Frames of Mind: The theory of multiple intelligences.*

This theory inspired me to create this book and analyze the correlation between intelligence types, success, and happiness. In the coming chapters, I will present all nine of Gardner's intelligence types. I will analyze the lives of successful people -- what is their motivation, and how did they achieve greatness? I will provide useful advice on how to improve each of these skills. Just as I wrote above, intelligence can be improved through learning and practice.

But first, let's see how Howard Gardner arrived at his thesis. He tested people with special skills and did anthropological measurements on subjects coming from different cultures. Based on the results of this research and biological facts obtained from visual and imagining procedures, he introduced eight (and eventually nine) intelligence categories.

- Linguistic and verbal intelligence (good with words)
- Logical - mathematical intelligence (good at math and solving logic problems)
- Visual - spatial intelligence (good with pictures)
- Body - movement intelligence (good at sports and movement)
- Musical intelligence (good at music and rhythm)
- Interpersonal intelligence (good with people and communication)

- Intrapersonal intelligence (good analyzing skills)
- Naturalist intelligence (good at understanding the natural world)
- Existential intelligence (good at understanding the supernatural world)

Originally he was working with seven intelligence types, but as years passed and he dug deeper in the topic, Gardner realized there is another intelligence type. People who are strongly connected with nature – with the flora, fauna and minerals – were sorted into a different category for naturalist intelligence. Connection with the environment can have a strong impact on our lives and can define a person totally. So starting in 1995, naturalist intelligence was introduced as the eighth type of intelligence.

In 1999 the author started considering a ninth intelligence, the existential intelligence. Gardner said this type of intelligence "scored reasonably well on the criteria" still very vague category so he never included it officially in his study. However, I decided to include it in my book as another type. Maybe somebody will feel a strong connection with this type of "intelligence."

Nowadays the emphasis is on the measurement of intrapersonal intelligence and kinesthetic intelligence. These two quotients can provide essential information that can be used in education and in the competitive labor market. The information acquired through the tests that measured the subject's ability to solve everyday tasks influenced the subject rankings. The improvement of these subject's abilities was found to be very useful, even indispensable in our accelerated, fast-paced world.

Some criticize Gardner's theory. One criticism is that of Gardner's "intelligences" are not necessarily a part of the cognitive sphere; they are skills rather than intelligence. Musical talent or kinesthetic skills are abilities.

Another criticism attacks the fact that Gardner's intelligences types are separate domains. The critics claim there is correlation between them. A ping-pong-style debate evolved after this attack. Gardner said the illusion of correlation is due to the format of IQ tests, which always require linguistic and logic skills. As a counterattack his critics pointed out that there are other types of IQ tests that measure spatial abilities, reaction time, and other basic cognitive tasks that don't involve logical or linguistic thinking.

Gardner's theory's other weak point is that the categories reflect more his intuition and reasoning than full, empirical research.

Regardless of who is right, one thing is true: Gardner's concept has been very useful in education. Many educators reflected on their teaching methods and broadened the perspective of their regular practices. They broadened their focus and concentrated on methods that might assist people in living their lives better.

And this is my goal as well. I strongly believe that a sharper focus on our strongest, best skills can help build self-esteem, contentment, and confidence. Focusing and improving your strength is a strategy that will continuously make you happy and successful.

If you want to prevail, if you seek success, improve yourself! Study! With the help of this book you will find out, which intelligence type defines you the best. Learn how to bring out the most in it.

Chapter 4: Linguistic and verbal intelligence

Communication and thought are the greatest differences between humans and animals. Everybody can speak or communicate in one way or another. We've been learning it since we were born.

However, there are some people who can do it better than others, they "have a way with words." They get along with others easily. They are charming, funny, can tell colorful stories and never seem like they'd run out of things to talk about.

If you already recognize yourself in the short description above, it is highly likely that verbal intelligence is your forte. Let's take a look at the main characteristics of this type of intelligence.

- You are a talented writer.
- You tell engaging stories.

- You're good with crossword puzzles.
- You like to participate in arguments – and usually win.
- You're considered to be funny.
- You give clear explanations.
- You have a great vocabulary and enjoy learning new words.
- You're good with foreign languages.

If you matched more than four, it is almost certain that you are gifted with verbal intelligence. Don't forget, people can excel in several intelligence types.

Verbal intelligence is a very complex category that we can break down into three subcategories or dialects.

1. **Spoken language**

   -*"I have a dream..."*

I don't need to say any more of this quote. Dr. Martin Luther King Jr.'s speech from the August 28, 1963 March on Washington for Jobs and Freedom is known worldwide. He was not only a great orator, but also a beloved public figure. He fought for the common cause of many by calling for the end of racism and equal civil and economic rights in the United States.

Apart from his unique presentation skills, Dr. Martin Luther King Jr. used some of his sentences repeatedly, and used some so-called anaphoras to emphasize his message. *I have a dream, now is the time,* and *free at last* are just a few key examples of messages he repeated when he addressed the public.

Being a good public speaker requires several skills. You have to have a powerful, charismatic air, good language; you have to present whatever you talk about in an engaging manner. You have to adapt your message to the audience – you present a topic differently to teenagers than to pensioners.

You must have an emotional impact on your audience. Based on what you are talking about, you must tap into people's main emotions like joy, hope, disgust, anger, and fear. You have to use vivid and descriptive words to make it easier for your audience to picture your stories.

Today, I admire stand up comedians. They have to seize the moment, capture the audience instantly, be super funny, present jokes in a colorful yet understandable manner, recover from failed jokes without hesitation, and they have to handle all of this in present time. If you want to improve your public speaking skills, I'd strongly suggest "stealing" some tricks from these guys. Also there is a growing trend in the

US for the people who wish to improve their public speaking skills to take improvisational comedy classes. Give it a try.

2. Hearing and comprehension

There are three parts to a language exam: written, oral, and listening comprehension. For the listening comprehension, the examiner puts in a CD and the student has to pick the right answers for the questions based on the text.

It is very interesting but this is the most commonly failed section of the test with the lowest scores. Why?

You could answer this question with a cliché: because people like to talk more than to listen. Nevertheless, it is true, but for good reason. Research from Lac Kong University of Vietnam proved that listening is often ignored in elementary through high school education worldwide. The greatest emphasis is on written language and then on spoken language.

It is important to practice listening exercises as much as possible. Good communication is bidirectional. It is not enough to spill out your message; it is also essential to understand the response. This includes the comprehension of the other person's speaking style, accent, pronunciation etc.

To improve listening and comprehending skills, it can be a good exercise to rephrase what our speaking partner has said. After he finishes his thread ask him:

- "By saying this did you mean..." - and summarize what you understood.

This exercise will not only improve your listening skills, but it will also leave your partner with the feeling that you were paying attention.

3. Written language

"There was no student in the entire institution with less of a military bearing than ... He moved clumsily and jerkily; his uniform hung awkwardly on him; and his knapsack, shako and rifle all looked like some sort of fetter he had been forced to wear for a time and which lay heavily on him."

The quote above is from *The Dostoevsky Encyclopedia* by K. A. Lantz, about one of the greatest Russian novelists, F. M. Dostoyevsky.

This is a perfect example of how not all professions are a good fit for everybody.

Dostoyevsky's father sent him to a military academy, but clearly he hated it. Body/movement intelligence was not his strong point.

What matters in this story is that Dostoyevsky started writing books at a young age and became one of the best character developers in the world. Critics also say he was one of the greatest psychologists in the world of literature. His success was due to his unique way of grabbing social dilemmas and presenting them with passion and conviction.

Some people might not be the best public speakers because even if they have all the material they need to put together a good speech with a clear message, they lack the charisma and courage to transmit it to the people. But maybe they can communicate the message in a written form.

To become a great writer, you ought to be a great reader. Read as many books you can in as many genres as possible. Reading will enrich your vocabulary, help you to get familiar with different writing styles, and broaden your knowledge of people and the world in general.

Find your audience, find YOUR core message and make sure this message benefits them, and that they'll care about what you write.

Some people possess talent for all three subcategories mentioned above, and some only possess talent for one or two. However, all of them can be improved. The person who has a natural skill in verbal intelligence can, with diligence, become great in all other dialects. Becoming a good public speaker or a great listener may take a lot of effort and persistence, but at the end of the day, it will be worth it.

If you master the intelligence type you are best at, you will have no problem happily making a living from it.

Chapter 5: Logical-mathematical intelligence

Cogito ergo sum!

I think, therefore I am. People with a strong logical and mathematical intelligence are considered to be quick-minded with good math skills and precise solutions for logic problems. They work easily with numbers, formulas that may appear abstract, shapes, and equations. They are able to prepare complex plans in little time. The creation and implementation of complex systems is not difficult for them.

The Greek giant, Archimedes of Syracuse, was one of the greatest mathematicians of the ancient world. He was a scientist, mathematician, physicist, engineer, astronomer, and philosopher from Sicily. He discovered buoyancy (Archimedes' principle) while bathing in a tub. Legend says that he was so carried away by enthusiasm that he jumped out of the bath and ran naked through the streets of Syracuse, shouting: "Eureka, eureka" (I found). And the results of his work affect our lives to this day.

Archimedes is considered the first mathematical physicist, before Galileo and Newton. He made his mark in the fields of mathematics, geometry, physics, and astronomy. The Archimedes screw was first used in Egypt for water-lifting machines. Nowadays this tool is used for the harvester-thresher machines as well.

Certain eras and cultures have left strong traces in the development and advancement of academic life. In ancient and medieval warfare advancements could have not been made without the inventions and great discoveries of engineers. Algebra was developed based on the usage of Arabic numerals. The Vikings brought the world advancements in shipbuilding and compass applications. The Portuguese and Spanish ships brought us the discovery of uncharted areas.

People gifted with this intelligence type tend to do abstract logical thinking without any special effort. At first discovery, Albert Einstein's famous theory of relativity would have been almost impossible for an ordinary person to follow.

People with strong logical and mathematical intelligence learn workflows faster than their peers. They have been interested in how things work since they were children. Many did things like take their little toy cars apart to see how they worked.

Some people learn to use computers and software easily, while others cannot grasp the basics. The technology world's greatest names are Bill Gates of Microsoft, Steve Jobs of Apple, and Mark Zuckerberg of Facebook among others. There are many others. Let's see if you have the potential to become one of them.

- Do you enjoy solving mysteries? Are

you good at strategy games?

- Can you solve logic problems and look for rational explanations?
- Are you good at and do you enjoy math?
- Do you like to organize things by category?
- Have you always been interested in scientific discoveries and experiments?
- Are you an abstract thinker?
- Do you wonder how things work?
- Are you good with computers? Do you have a mind "like a computer?"

Few people are as financially successful as those with high logical and mathematical intelligence. The members of the Rothschild family or Gates family are the representatives of the modern age.

The last Lydian king, Croesus, who lived in ancient times minted gold and silver coins to create currency. He was a great conqueror and legendarily rich king who understood the language of money well.

But the wealth poisoned his mind and logical thinking thus caused his downfall. According to the legend, he asked Apollo if he should launch a campaign against the Persians and if he did what the outcome would be. He received the following response: "If you attack Persia, a great empire will collapse." He thought Apollo was talking about Persia, but he was talking about Croesus' own kingdom...

If you are blessed with logical and mathematical intelligence, you may have already analyzed the pros and cons of this gift, the possibilities and hindrances around you, and you may know exactly what you want. Now I will help you with the *how*.

1. **Start easy: learn games that require logical intelligence.**

Learn to play chess or use an abacus, and make it sure to practice often. There are lots of books, videos, and techniques you can learn to bring out your own style.

Play at least one of them weekly. Make it a routine, on Saturday from ten to twelve play chess. On Friday from five to six read something about chess that you'll try the next day.

2. **Take some math, science and/or computer programming courses.**

Your brain craves new information. In the field of logic and math there is always more to learn. There are universal truths like 2+2=4, but there is so much more. And there are the ever-changing fields like informatics.

It isn't greedy or lazy to invest in yourself by taking a course that will broaden your knowledge. There is this wonderful fact about knowledge: once it is yours, nobody can take away.

3. Use deductive thinking.

I think all of us would like to be Sherlock Holmes from time to time. Good news, you could actually be a pretty good one. Make up theories in your mind and try to solve them. Read and watch detective stories. Then make up you own story. Imagine you're the detective of a whodunit. It will not only broaden your deductive thinking, but it will also be fun. Who said logic had to be boring?

4. Read the business sections of newspaper – and do the Sudoku in the back.

Being aware of the business world is a must for those who want to work in this field. Banking, stock market changes, hedge funds, and economic charts are just a small part of the information you should follow. Some say knowledge is power. In this field definitely! Also, you can bring your practice from number three (above) to the next level here by deducing real-life possibilities. Make predictions, analyze, and interpret data and statistics.

5. Brain + heart.

It's ok to think with your heart from time to time. It's not ruining your mastermind reputation. It will help you understand some correlations better.

Some people think emotions ruin rational thinking. But believing that we can exclude emotions is totally irrational. We are logical emotional beings. One cannot live happily without the other. Even the greatest logical minds, the most materialistic businessmen, fall to their knees in the face of some emotional beauty or sadness. Get to know the emotional side of your coin as well. Even if you do not agree with some, accept that others see that event in a less logical and more emotional way. If you accept this variety in human nature, you'll be much better at deductive thinking as well.

Like our bodies, the mind must be maintained! Like we build the body, we must build the mind too! Reading, learning, and practice can increase the level of logical

mathematical intelligence!

Chapter 6: Visual-spatial intelligence

Everyone has heard of Michelangelo and Leonardo da Vinci, who were prominent members of the Italian Renaissance. Michelangelo is best known for his David statue and the Sistine Chapel's ceiling fresco that immortalized his name. Leonardo da Vinci painted the Mona Lisa and The Last Supper.

Antoni Gaudi, the Catalan architect, is closely linked to Barcelona. Gustave Eiffel designed and built the Eiffel Tower of Paris and the internal structure of New York's Statue of Liberty.

Thor Heyerdahl, a Norwegian ethnographer, concluded in his research that the ancestors of the Polynesian natives lived in South America before they sailed across the Pacific Ocean to the modern-day Polynesia. This assumption was proven to be true by the Kon-Tiki expedition he managed and organized. Without a high degree of spatial intelligence, it would have been impossible to build a seaworthy balsa wood raft sufficient to make the trip like he did. Celestial navigation requires a special ability not only from the navigator, but also from the helmsman. In that age especially, imagining the location of the ship or raft under the stars was a challenging job.

Now it is much easier with the sextant and global positioning systems (GPS).

Every man is born with high intelligence. This intelligence is never used to its full potential. Imitating our parents, family members, and environment we are stuck using certain abilities, a fraction of what we could be. Why? Because this is what we've learned. Because it's easier. The mechanical learning of the "modern" education system stifles the mind's activity. Our abilities and opportunities are minimally used.

People who think in images, colors, and graphics have good spatial vision, in other words good visual and spatial intelligence.

A spatial, problem-solving ability is essential for navigation and map creation. Also in chess when you have to foresee the combinations of possible moves -- not only on the chessboard. In architecture it is also essential, when an object or objects have to be described, then edited, and drawn or created, to see a structure in all three dimensions. Spatial intelligence is also needed in painting and in sculpture and other visual art forms.

Do you posses some of the following qualities?

- You are good in putting puzzles together.
- You enjoy art and photography.
- You prefer geometry over algebra.
- You study with charts and pictures.
- You're good with directions, and can find your way with a map.
- You can visualize pictures in your head, and notice colors and shapes.

- You're good at doodling or drawing.
- You can remember places vividly.

How do you train yourself to succeed in this field?

1. **The brain must be "heated".**

   It is a simple change we can make in our everyday actions. In the mornings, in the evenings - during the day and after meals - we brush our teeth. Starting today let's use the other hand, with which we have not carried out this operation until now. Due to the unexpected and unfamiliar change the brain starts to rebel and quit the sweet routine operations and will start to focus. So it gets "heated". Later we can do more complicated changes to "heat" our brain.

2. **Visualize by reading.**

   Give yourself 15-20 minutes of reading time everyday. Read any kind of book, magazine, or comics. Then draw out what you read. On the bottom right (or left) corner of the paper write the date. Don't get discouraged if the picture is not a complex technical drawing. It is enough to recall what you read later in the week.

Recall your favorite childhood tales and stories. Draw them. Think of a short story and draw a conceptual map. Again, it shouldn't be a super high-quality map, just sufficient to demonstrate the plot.

Important! DO NOT GIVE UP! Do it and practice it! A week later your drawing will be better than it is now. After a month it will take less time and be more transparent. Be persistent! DO NOT GIVE UP!

Do not cheat! Do it for yourself. Nobody will see your work if you don't want them to. There's nothing to be ashamed of. You practice, you improve something that will make you a better professional, and, through persistence, a better person.

3. **Dare to go big.**

    Put your dream house on paper. Leave the computer-aided design programs for later. They can come into play in the polishing stage. In the meantime, dream up and draw down how it will look on the inside. Let your fantasies free: visualize your dream garden with all the plants, different trees, and garden furniture. Now start to see the spring and autumn colors surrounding your home. Draw in what you'd like to see in the virtual space. Then you can use a computer program to refine the plans.

4. **Fire the GPS.**

    You're travelling. You sit in the car and the GPS is on. Mute the sound of the navigator and replace it by reading the route map. It's a good exercise. At first use a well-known route that you know almost by heart.

Then move the exercise to the next level and instead of a GPS, use a printed map to get directions. Search for the best route before departing. Then be your own navigator! It is time to learn this.

5. **Visual forecaster.**

Put a tape measure in your pocket. Walk down the street and select an object (something big enough to embrace), and try to guess its dimensions. How many inches is it in length or width or height? Then measure it. Was there a big difference between your estimate and the actual measurement? Choose another object and do the same thing. Then another, and then a few more. Don't change the process. After a while your estimates will get closer to the actual size.

Another practice. How many steps am I away from the building or the stop sign? Guess. Then count your steps! Keep practicing. So you can develop the accuracy of your estimates.

Remember, do not give up!

Chapter 7: Body - movement intelligence

Athleticism requires exceptional coordination and grace along with unmatched mental game and competitiveness. Like Michael Jordan, the greatest basketball player of all time, who didn't just play, but literally reinvented basketball.

This athletic genius dropped out of his school's basketball team. If you've read my previous books, you might expect me to write something about grit and persistence. Not this time. This time I'm going to focus simply on the super talent factor of this equation. He is a person who combined his innate skills with diligence to master the art of movement.

Some people were born to move. Check the list below to see how many of the following general characteristics match you. If at least four, there is a good chance you are, like MJ, gifted with this intelligence.

- You're good at sports.
- You can dance well.
- You learn by doing.
- You "talk" and work with your hands.
- You're interested in acting.
- You like to build things.
- You're well coordinated and have good motor skills.
- You can't sit still for too long.

People forget things easily. Just try to remember what you did last Wednesday. Right? Unless your child was born, you got your first tattoo, or you met the love of your life, you probably won't remember it too clearly. But maybe you never forget biking. There's this saying about everything related to motion: "it's like riding a bike, once you've learned it you never forget."

This is what we call kinesthetic memory. In other words, the procedure to learn and remember things through motion. But even in kinesthetic learning there are "dialects." People have different memory systems and based on these differences they learn through different types of motions.

There are whole body learners, doodlers, hands-on learners, and people who learn through emotional experiences. Not everything is like the kinesthetic learning of biking. There are some things, which you remember short-term, however there are different techniques to plant these newly learned things into your long-term memory.

1. **Whole body learning:**

   People gifted with this dialect of movement intelligence learn the best and quickest if they use their whole body actively. They can bring out the most of their potential by role-playing, doing puzzles, body mappings, using computer technology (YouTube for example) to learn certain movements, or computer accessory tools that require movements (like a wheel to Need for Speed).

Regardless of whether you want to act, be a long-distance runner, or be a first-class computer game player, you need your body and mind to be synchronized. Repetition is the key to learning something and moving it to your long-term memory.

2. **Doodlers**:

If whole body learners are on one side of the coin, doodlers are on the other. Doodlers have very high motion intelligence as well, but they learn by designing things. The best way for them to learn and retain something in long-term memory is to mind-map, draw, story map, etc.

If whole body learners are the players on the field, the doodler is the coach. Doodlers are exceptionally good at creating strategies that are applicable to motion. You don't have to picture them as football coaches, but dance choreographers, architects, and physical therapists.

3. **Hands on learners**:

There are those people who are not afraid of heavy physical work; they may even enjoy it. They can be talented mechanics, successful body builders, good craftsmen, or even firefighters.

The best way to retain learning related to body movement is to role-play, use clay, build, and do every type of exercise that requires heavy manual work. If you feel talented in this regard, you can maximize your potential by exploring all the possibilities of your profession. Develop your manual dexterity.

If you are a good mechanic, read about new technologies and try to implement them. If you find something useful for your job, set aside one hour every day to practice that one thing until you can do it easily, until it becomes a subconscious reflex for you. It can also help if you try out totally new things. Start learning to play the piano, paint, or weave.

4. **People who learn through emotional experiences**:

These people don't learn by doing a motion, but by the emotions a particular motion triggers in them. That's why it is important for emotional learners to maximize their potential by doing things they really enjoy. Some people are able to do stuff they don't enjoy much because they know if they pass that stage they'll be much better.

Emotional learners are not like this. If they hate something, they HATE it. That's it. So they should use techniques that really are in balance with their emotional background. These can be role-plays, dramas, charades, or debates. Emotional learners are usually actors, performers, and other types of public entertainers like politicians (OK, just joking).

We have to make an important distinction between gross motor skills and fine motor skills. The former is responsible for big range motions using our arms, legs, and body. Almost everybody has an innate ability to acquire gross motor skills usually in early childhood. We learn to walk, run, stand up, and climb stairs – and, eventually, biking to stick with the previous example. Gross motor skills are those we won't forget easily.

Fine motor skills are used in more delicate motions that involve our hands, fingers, feet, and toes. These motions can range from learning how to pick up a fork to drawing a picture like Michelangelo's The Last Judgment. Gross and fine motor skills combine to be responsible for coordination.

So good news, if you're talented with kinesthetic intelligence, with practice you can master sculpture just as you've mastered eating with a fork and a knife. It's not something you can learn overnight, but with practice you have a good chance of being pretty good.

How do we motivate people with kinesthetic intelligence?

Most of them are competitive, full of energy and possess a strong desire to create. So the best way to keep them motivated is to appoint new challenges for them – long- and short-term ones. When they complete a challenge they have to feel they improved by doing it. They learned and made a step forward.

It is also important to give a clear explanation of the consequences if a task is not done well or if it is overdone. Some people tend to overdo things. They are called hyperactive although I really hate this word. I think lazy people invented the term because they were envious of their energy. (This is a non-scientific explanation from a person who has often been labeled hyperactive. Don't give it much credit. No more jokes, back to the science.) Hyperactive people tend to overdo things. They need a different kind of motivation than normal or less-motivated people. They need regular monitoring, clear directions, and clear boundaries wherein they can act freely.

And if the task is successfully completed these people should be rewarded. If the task is not properly completed or the expectations aren't met this time, the worst thing one can do is to punish. On one hand it is counterintuitive. If people try and fail and then get scolded, it's very possible they won't even try the next time. You won't get the desired result if you punish. Studies show that animals learn things much quicker and retain the knowledge for longer when they are offered more treats than punishment.

This is also true if you motivate yourself. Reward yourself when you complete a task. A small task earns a small reward, and a big task earns a big reward. Punishment should be avoided. This rule applies for all types of intelligence not only kinesthetic.

Chapter 8: Musical intelligence

Your soul is the melody, your body is the rhythm, and your mind is the rhyme.

I heard this thought a few years ago. A flash sprung up from the depths of my memory because it's very apt here.

The seeds of musical intelligence are in every newborn's brain, but they only grow if they're exposed to external stimuli. The children who perform at a high level in this area or have an affinity for music point in this direction. It is likely that sounds and rhythms in some form will be part of their lives.

We start to hear sooner than to see, speak, or walk. Nature created us like this. Some people are tone-deaf, some have good hearing, some relative hearing, and some people are blessed with absolute hearing. The latter is an innate talent of a select few people. Relatively good hearing can be developed with practice. Many musicians learn this skill. People with good hearing don't need to feel ashamed because at parties, weddings, or simply singing a song for fun, they hold their own. Tone-deaf people are probably gifted with another intelligence and would be more successful in that area.

In the first few months of infancy, a child's ability to make music is displayed next to the aforementioned detection processes. Babies babble indicating that they're receptive to rhythms, and melodies. It can be observed that until the age of two, this ability can develop into making up small songs and poems. The blabbing and giggling is typical for this stage of life.

However what is the percentage of instinctive musical talent and inherited abilities in these cases? To what extent is this intelligence innate and how much can be developed?

Musical intelligence is not only a product of the environment in which we grew up, but also inherited from our family, and cultural heritage.

We could summarize the nature of musical intelligence this way: musical intelligence is the ability to sing well, to compose, and to play musical instruments. With this type of intelligence, you can build a future.

Musical intelligence is independent but still has an impact on the other varieties of intelligence. Research has shown that music goes through other tests of intelligence as well.

Musical intelligence is largely dependent on personal development, musical training, and practice.

Music is personality forming. So are you musically intelligent?

- Do you have good rhythm?

- Can you read music and are you talented with an instrument or your voice?
- Do you criticize new songs?
- Are you often singing, whistling, or tapping along to a song?
- Can you can figure out how to play a tune on an instrument?
- Have you considered writing songs?
- Can you tell when a note is off-key?
- Can you remember old songs, and easily memorize songs?

If you have at least four of these traits above, you're in a serious danger of being blessed with musical intelligence.

The mapping of musical intelligence also discovered that different personality types like different styles of music. Musical tastes may affect the way we think about our daily habits, our actions, and even the way we dress. It is awkward if someone mocks or insults your favorite band or style of music. You feel attracted to a certain type of music because deep down you connect with it in some way.

A professor at Cambridge University, Peter Rentfrow found a strong correlation between musical taste and personality. Professor Rentfrow and professor Sam Gosling at the University of Texas defined four categories:

- **Reflexive / complex** (classical, jazz, blues, folk). Classical music lovers are characterized as intelligent, literate, and tolerant. They have exquisite taste, spiritual sensitivity, are at peace with themselves, and rarely feel unsatisfied. Jazz lovers are more assertive and strong. Blues and soul lovers form a lighter, gentler category.

- **Rhythmic / energetic** (hip-hop, dance). People who like this style of music do not care if it is sunny, raining, or perhaps even a raging blizzard. They are characterized as confident, liberal thinkers. They like the company of others but also enjoy being alone. They are active and passive participants in sports that play an important role in their lives. Satisfied with their outlook, they don't care much about others' opinions.

- **Amusement / traditional** (pop, country). Pop and country music lovers are confident, diligent in their work, and love to help others. At some level, they are characterized by a rather conservative attitude. They are open and honest. It is important for them to maintain customs and traditions. Even though they have a strong self-esteem, they can often feel dissatisfied with themselves.

- **Intensive / rebel** (heavy metal, rock,

alternative rock, rap). Fans of this music are usually sporty, energetic, and adventurous. Always looking for new and special challenges, they can be characterized as curious and intelligent. Rap lovers have great self-confidence, maybe even too much sometimes. Generally they are open, friendly with people, and eager to seek the company of others.

The brain center responsible for the perception of music and composition is located in the right hemisphere. However, the sections in charge of musical abilities cannot be demarked very clearly.

A musically talented person is often also a good dancer and singer. It is also true that not all good dancers are good singers, no matter how excellent their musical talent. What they have in common is a sense of rhythm.

How can musical intelligence be improved?

1. **Practice, practice, and practice.**

   It doesn't matter what area of the music and rhythm field you want to improve, practice is key. You dance? Dance more. You sing? Sing more. You compose? Compose more. I could really blab a few more paragraphs full of reasons, but I'll conclude with this one word: PRACTICE.

2. **Learn and exercise with music.**

   Some people are said to be visual types when it comes to learning. A person with musical intelligence is more the audio type. They should attach music to different subjects when they learn them. Listen to the same melody for the same topic. When the exam comes they can just recall the melody and remember the subject as well. Also, these people can use rap to memorize lists and course materials.

Music can boost your physical resistance too. When you hear your favorite music your blood starts to pump quicker and your performance endurance will increase. This rule applies for everybody, not only those who are not particularly gifted with musical intelligence.

3. Try out different fields of musical intelligence.

Are you a singer? Try to write a song or join a dance group. Are you a dancer? Try choreography. The more fields you explore, the bigger your experience and expertize will become. At the end of the day all these fields are connected through rhythm. Whatever you do, your sense of rhythm will improve. Make the most of it!

If you feel vulnerable or incomplete and fear those many hours of practice won't pay off, just remember this.

Beethoven's Third Symphony was presented in 1805 and a milestone in music history. Beginning in 1802, the artist gradually began to lose hearing and still managed to compose the Ninth Symphony when he was totally deaf. This, nor any of his previous work could have been written without years of utter and diligent practice.

So do not give up! Practice, believe, and be patient. It will pay off.

Chapter 9: Interpersonal intelligence

If I say the names Mother Theresa, Princess Diana, and Oprah Winfrey, what is the first word that pops into your mind? Maybe something like kind-hearted, empathic, "a people person," or famous in the best sense of the word. All of this is true.

People with strong interpersonal intelligence can easily understand others' feelings and motivations. They have a strong sense of empathy and justice, and they are not afraid to share their opinions with others. They like giving advice and listening to people's problems. A person with interpersonal intelligence attracts others who want to share their problems.

If you think that more than four of the following qualities describe you, it's highly possible your interpersonal intelligence is quite high.

- You can often read others' minds.

- You have a strong sense of justice.
- You're a good listener.
- You have a well-developed "lie detector."
- You enjoy being around others.
- You have good problem-solving skills.
- You are empathetic.
- You are skilled in verbal and nonverbal communication.

Traditionally, there are more women than men who have interpersonal intelligence as their strongest intelligence. Women can read body language more intuitively; they can express and so understand others people's feelings better.

How can interpersonal intelligence be measured? The author of the first book written on the topic of multiple intelligence, Dr. Howard Gardner, equalized interpersonal intelligence with Goleman's emotional intelligence. EI (or EQ) can be measured with several tests based on the traditional IQ tests. But here emotion-based problem-solving skills are emphasized. Some question these tests' accuracy and their capacity to measure the level of intelligence citing a lack of objectively correct answers. Since the answers are based on emotion, it is impossible to create questions with clearly right or wrong answers.

Anyway, my point here is not to decide whether EI tests are accurate or not, but to get you to think about it. You all can decide for yourselves if you want to give credit to the EI tests. I personally think that EI, or any kind of test that we do, is just an opportunity for feedback about your current intelligence level in that particular area. I believe everything can be improved. You should focus on the hows not the whys. In other words, use "how can I evolve?" instead of "why did I get this score?" or "why am I not better at...?"

Remember, change is bidirectional – you can change for the better or for worse. But evolvement or improvement indicates a positive direction, always higher than before.

So how can you improve your interpersonal intelligence?

People who have a strong interpersonal intelligence are more extroverted, love teamwork, team sports, and are social butterflies. They feel comfortable among people and don't mind getting to know strangers. They have many friends or close acquaintances. They would like to meet as many people as possible during their days, but must be careful not to neglect other responsibilities. Many interpersonal people are spontaneous but a little disorganized. So my first tips for them are these:

1. **Get organized**. Keep your schedule in a calendar or booklet. Explore and establish a time-management system that allows you to do as many of your favorite activities as you want but still allows you to fulfill your

everyday requirements.

Also, make sure to keep in touch with your network. Take the time to meet with all the important people around you regularly (weekly or every two weeks). If several people are equally important to you, give them equal time so you can to save yourself from an unwanted sense of guilt.

2. **Practice listening**. People with a strong interpersonal intelligence are not only natural connection-makers, but also good listeners. However, just as making a great connection needs practice, so does deep listening. Luckily for you, opportunities to improve this skill are countless. Since you are always surrounded with people, just decide to dedicate your time and focus on the person you are with. Decide that in the next thirty minutes you will only listen to your spouse, child, or friend.

Think through what they are talking about, if there is a hidden message behind their words. Do not interrupt them, maintain eye contact, nod if they need encouragement. If they stop, count to three before you ask a question or reflect your own opinion. Maybe they are just thinking about how to go on. You can give positive feedback to them in two ways. One way is to ask more about their problem. Another way is to rephrase what they said with your own words – this will show that you are listening and avoid misunderstandings.

3. **Use different channels to communicate with people.** This way you'll not only broaden your knowledge of how to handle conversations in different areas, but also get to know many kinds of people. What I mean: have face-to-face meetings everyday or a few times a week with people you are fond of. Also have some pen pals – if they are from different countries, even better.

You can enjoy interesting conversations and get a perspective about how people think about the same ideas on a different side of the globe. Go to events where you don't know everybody – so you can improve your "first impression" charisma.

4. **Make learning a hobby**. Regardless of whether your main job is strongly connected with interpersonal intelligence or not, find time to practice. Participate in workshops and/or seminars that are communication related. Find a hobby that involves meeting like-minded people. Listen and share. A learning process can have two directions: one is when you listen and absorb new information, the other is when you share your knowledge and teach others.

5. **Meditate about your connections**. Sometimes even the most social person needs time to withdraw and analyze the

events and people. Take the time to contemplate the week's events once a week, maybe Sunday. Think about who you met, what conversations you had. Did it improve or destroy your relationship? Was there a mistake? Where? What were the best parts of the conversation? Where can you build that specific relationship in the future? After this, make a meeting schedule (see point 1) for the next week. And start practicing points 1-5 all over again.

The five points above are good ways to improve your interpersonal intelligence, bring out the most of your extraverted skills, and, with practice, eventually become a master communicator and connection-maker.

Interpersonal intelligence is important if you are working as a diplomat, manager, clergy, social worker, but also if you are a sales person, coach, or politician. All professions fit you if they require engagement with people.

A last piece of advice for you, my interpersonal intelligence-heavy friend: understand many, but react to only a few. In other words, do not let others ruin your mood. When I arrived in a new community at fourteen I was very energetic, jumpy with a let's-do-it attitude. But I had to realize the others around me were simply not like that. And I was, "oh, no? ok... well..." And I repressed my burning desire to get to know people for a time in an effort to blend in until I met somebody who was just like me.

It is good to meet as many people as possible, but learn to accept that not all of them think as you do. Do not take it personally. Listen to them, make notes about their behavior, don't judge them, but also you do not have to identify with them. Just because you can't make a super connection with them, it doesn't mean something's wrong with you. It means the two of you think on different wavelengths. What you can do is choose to spend most of your time with like-minded people who help you and enforce this strength in you.

I also wouldn't suggest avoiding the other group of people. It is important to know how to handle as many types of people as possible. But do not take their problems and words personally.

Being empathic and sensible, you can get emotionally hurt quite easily because you feel strongly. Build up a self-protection system. When you start feeling somebody is touching your soul "with dirty hands" just repeat this:

> *This is not about me. This person is uneasy with him/herself. I love myself! I feel good! I know who I am!*

Chapter 10: Intrapersonal intelligence

Intrapersonal intelligence helps people detect and understand their own emotions. Humans are no longer living on instincts anymore, but we have risen to the intellectual-emotional level. Now we have to learn how to cohabitate with the environment and ourselves. If we're at peace with the latter, we won't have big issues with the former.

This is an ability (intelligence) that helps us discover our motivations and emotions objectively. Our inner world is what we reflect to others. When we make connections with other people through human relations and everyday activities, we have to know how to handle and control our feelings.

An individual's everyday life is strongly influenced by the components of intrapersonal and interpersonal intelligence. There's a theory that 80 percent of a person's success depends on inter- and intrapersonal intelligence. These two intelligences together make up our emotional intelligence. The remaining 20 percent is made up of other intelligence types. The authenticity of these assumptions has not yet been proven in any literature's factual findings. Your practical experience will prove or disprove this hypothesis.

But the fact that well-developed intra- and interpersonal intelligence can remarkably improve personal relationships is indisputable. Just like how understanding our own emotional motivations helps us accept ourselves and others.

People with strong intrapersonal intelligence can be characterized as strong-willed and determined; they know themselves. They are aware of their abilities. They walk the walk because they've found their purpose in life. They've set goals and targets they want to reach. They are self-confident and this confidence emanates from the knowledge of their own abilities. They are able to learn from their mistakes and successes as well. They are independent and prefer to act alone.

People with high intrapersonal intelligence are usually philosophers, poets, novelists, mystics, counselors, songwriters, and psychologists. People with a deep sense of self.

Psychology is one of the professions where individuals with advanced intrapersonal intelligence are frequently represented. They have an ability to detect, localize, and resolve psychological problems. Most of them chose this path to learn more about themselves, their issues, and then help others with similar problems.

Many people can't detect the small quivers of the human soul. They simply do not develop the ability. This is not a problem for others. These perceptions are absolutely natural. They can tune their brains quite simply to the vibrations, feelings, and signals flowing their way. They interpret and evaluate them.

Below are the characteristics that best describe this type of intelligence.

- You have deep self-knowledge, and you're also self-critical.
- You're aware of your own feelings.
- You have a well-developed sense of self and honor your values.
- You have a strong awareness of your purpose in life.
- You have good intuitive abilities.
- You're analytical.
- You are a unique and private person.
- You don't like to go with the flow.

If at least half of the criterion above apply to you, your intrapersonal intelligence is above average. You can create a real picture of yourself and it's much different from your family members' and friends' biased opinions.

Autism is a manifestation of intrapersonal intelligence. Autistic people have impaired intrapersonal intelligence. They cannot see their own personalities so clearly. Let me share an example.

Many of you have probably seen the movie *Mercury Rising*. Art Jeffries (Bruce Willis) is a disillusioned FBI agent on the verge of a nervous breakdown. Simon Lynch is a nine-year-old autistic boy who, through a unique combination of capabilities, deciphers the US military's secret code, the Mercury. This is an extremely complex cryptographic code. It was said that no human or computer could crack the code. As a test it was created to protect the United States' most important secrets. The creators hid the solution in a secret phone number in a puzzle magazine. The experts said the code couldn't be deciphered. Simon called this phone number.

The secret has to be kept. Simon's parents are killed and the child himself is in danger. Art finds the little boy and behind the fear he can see the reflection of his own spiritual world. When you have nothing to lose, isolation can provide strength. It is interesting and educational to follow of the personality development of the two main characters in this movie.

Intrapersonal intelligence is a dominant part of our personality. It's a set of features of individual personality traits. A healthy personality is characterized by several criteria.

Let's see how we strengthen our intrapersonal intelligence.

1. **Get to know yourself.**

   To develop intrapersonal intelligence you need to know yourself better! You can start by doing personality tests. Know where you stand! Keep a log that describes your day-to-day thoughts. Then periodically check the log for the details from your past.

Acknowledge what changed, what's the same, and what's better. Meditate to get closer to your own feelings and thoughts.

2. **Find a hobby that sets you far from the crowd**.

    People with a high intrapersonal intelligence are usually introverts. The following saying applies to them: "We have two ears and one mouth so that we can listen twice as much as we speak." Thus they prefer hobbies where they can be alone or where they do not have to interact too much.

    This hobby can be reading biographies or self-help books out in nature. Find a place where you can be totally relaxed and get into a meditative mood.

3. **Set long and short term personality goals for yourself**.

Think about the qualities you'd like to improve in yourself. Imagine yourself being that person. Visualize the benefits of this evolution, then think about the cognitive and actionable steps you have to make in order to achieve the desired skill.

Keep a notebook for recording the steps. Every evening write two or three things you have to do the next day to practice the quality you want to improve. Also, in the evening write down what you did or did not achieve from the previous day's plan. Meditate about it. Why did or didn't you accomplish something? How did you feel doing them? Write everything down so you can reread it anytime.

4. **Write your own autobiography or book.**

Often in childhood we report certain events differently to our parents or teachers. In adulthood we do the same with our friends or bosses. This skill can be taken to the next level and it can even provide a livelihood. There are people who are really born to write, but their propensity for writing has not yet been discovered.

Some people may have not yet realized that everything they do or say has an impact on other people. Train and develop this quality and put your ideas in a book. At first only a few people will listen, but gradually, more and more people will come.

Everybody can philosophize and share ideas. If you have a talent for it, why not give it a chance and do it more openly? Create your own framework of ideas. By working in your own system your sense of security may increase. If you train yourself, there is a good chance you can make a living from it.

You have the skill to recognize and change your behavior, build upon your strengths, and improve your weaknesses. You can develop yourself in a shorter period of time than others and can be goal-orientated in a more focused manner.

Chapter 11: Naturalist intelligence

There was a man in England who at the age of eight started to collect shells and minerals and took long walks to observe the environment. At the age of thirteen, he began assisting his brother in a chemistry lab. His father wanted him to become a doctor, but he disliked the medicine university and left it after two years. Instead, he continued his studies in natural science with the geology faculty. Between 1831 and 1836 he participated in a shipping expedition and conducted geological research in South America. Among his main theories he devised the theories of evolution, natural selection, and selective breeding. He is the author of the book, *The Descent of Man*, where he presents the theory of human being descendent from apes. Yes, this man is Charles Darwin, the greatest naturalists of all time.

Naturalistic Intelligence, by definition, is the ability

to find patterns in nature and work in a natural environment with animals, wildlife, and plants.

People who have a strong naturalistic intelligence love spending time outside. They love hiking, camping, gardening, taking care of animals etc. The most fitting professions for them are as geologists, marine biologists, farmers, zookeepers, ecologists, veterinarians, gardeners, etc.

These types of people have a great sensitivity to nature-related issues like pollution and animal cruelty. They divide the living things (animals, plants) from other features of nature (minerals, rocks, waters...), but they show a keen interest in protecting or discovering both.

If you have a Charles Darwin lost somewhere inside you, at least four of the following qualities will apply to you.

- You have a broad knowledge of nature.
- You are sensitive to ecology

and environmental and animal abuse.

- You see patterns in nature.
- You have a keen sense of balance with nature and your body.
- You choose to be a vegetarian.
- You read about nature and explorers.
- You prefer nature to cities.
- You feel the best in nature.

Do you feel quite a few of these characteristics define you? Then you should explore this talent of yours a bit more.

How do you improve your naturalistic intelligence?

1. Observe nature around you.

When I was a kid – it's debatable whether this was a long or short time ago – winters were long and cold with a lot of snow. I still remember my grandpa pulling the sled and taking me out to play in the snow. This however, has changed in the past fifteen years. It snows seldom and often Christmas day is warmer than it is in May. I do not know much about the science of it, but I do have an empirical base of comparison.

If discovering nature is your passion, do not hesitate to make some notes about it. If you see or experience something weird or uncommon, write it down. As the years progress you'll have more and more interesting facts to compare and analyze. It's a long process, but it's worth it. It's like keeping a journal of your feelings; it is good to read your thoughts five years later.

2. **Hands on.**

People with naturalist intelligence love to be outdoors most of the time. Depending on what you have an affinity for, you could choose a new hobby to pass the time.

If you are into plants and you don't have a

direct connection with animals, but you'd like to help them, you can get involved by volunteering to help care for wildlife. Time spent in the forest together with likeminded people, foresters, and other naturalists, could give you a boost for the weeks to come. Nature heals, and if you heal it in return, you'll feel a sense of enjoyment.

If you love animals and you'd like to spend more time with them but you can't have a pet (or you have a pet but it's still not enough), you can assist at the local zoo, animal shelter, or farm – whatever you have in your area. By connecting with animals, you'll feel a sense of completeness and helping somebody (even if it has four legs) releases a lot of positive energy.

Do you like to be outside in your community? Help out in local parks and gardens. Plant flowers or trees, pick up litter, repaint the benches, these are all useful and relaxing activities that give back to your community.

3. Zoom in.

Like, literally. If you are more fascinated by microbiology, the cellular function of beings, buy a microscope, binoculars, or a telescope. Study the skies, plants, minerals, and soils. Take notes about your observations.

Join a science or research group with a similar profile and discuss your analyses with the professors or other students.

I presented the three options above as part-time activities or hobbies, but any of them can become main activities in your life, and even provide a livelihood. It is never too early or to late to improve naturalist intelligence.

I have a friend from San Francisco who recently retired. He is sixty-five years old. He worked as an engineer all his life but has recently decided he wants to make a change. He decided to enroll at one of the local universities to get a degree in archeology, and now he researches genetic changes in cells. He wants to become a professor. I repeat: he is sixty-five. He is so amazing and inspiring!

Think small or big about environmental involvement, both make a great difference. If every human in the world would pick up litter, plant some flowers and trees, and wouldn't consume so many natural resources (water, energy), we would live in a much better and cleaner world.

Chapter 12: Existential intelligence

"If an atheist and a pope think the same thoughts, it means that there is something that is true. There should be a human truth that exists regardless of religions." Until humanity has reached this recognition has lived through long centuries of trials and tribulations. This is a good starting point for the study and exploration of this subject. The quote comes from Oriana Fallaci, an Italian writer and journalist.

At the beginning, because of a lack of explanation, natural phenomena were attributed to powerful forces or spirits. People learned how to make fire, by calling on the God of Fire for help. For a successful hunt they had to seek the favor of the spirit that guided the animals. Then they had to placate the spirit of the prey. An unsuccessful hunt resulted in a different kind of atonement ceremony.

According to many, existential intelligence is the capability that best defines people. By contrast, in the academic world studies of the soul and spirit are not taken seriously and considered to be unfounded.

Where human life exists, there is existential intelligence. We leave this world with what our souls lived and experienced. These are not tangible, three-dimensional values. The soul is immortal; the body is mortal.

Human civilization and society has only been able to evolve and move forward when someone has violated the rules. True, the offender had to prove he was right, because if not ... retaliation came. Many times retaliation came even in spite of the evidence. At first they became the protagonists of a human sacrifice – in accordance with the habits of the era. Then leaders refined the rules and began to develop consequent penalties - law. They wanted to break the soul not just the body. Inquisition, anyone?

It has been a long road from the fire god to the organized religions of today. The established religions have some common features -- they seek questions and answer them, they explain how people were created and the purpose of their existence, they show other forms of existence. This is a very simplified idea.

Atheism is the belief in the absence of God or other supernatural forces. Some of the best known philosophers and thinkers - Marx, Nietzsche, and Freud – have said that people believe in God and the supernatural because they are afraid of death. It gives them a sense of security. The fear of punishment and otherworldly rewards influence their actions.

The existential intelligence is the most controversial of the intelligence types. To answer in-depth questions concerning human existence assumes a sensitivity to these issues. They try to answer such questions as:

- What is the origin of the universe?
- How did life on Earth appear?
- How did mankind appear?
- What is the meaning of life?
- Why do we die?
- Is there life after death?
- Is there a cosmic experience of unconditional love?
- What is the sense of happiness?

A small group of people, philosophers, are interested in unfolding the questions of existentialism. Here I take a science-based approach. Anthroposophy is the study of wisdom and knowledge in humans. It is the doctrine of man's knowledge based on philosophical principles.

Rudolf Steiner was a philosopher, writer, teacher, dramaturge, and the creator of a spiritual movement called anthroposophy. He is also the founder of Waldorf Education. This is a people-centered pedagogy, in which the child's talent for certain activities, teaching methods, and curriculum determines the lessons.

Every culture has developed their questions and self-explanatory systems. Regardless of the culture there are common features. These commonalities have emerged and started differentiating only in the course of time during the dawn of humanity.

How do we develop this abstract and colorful intelligence?

1. **We are many. Accept it and get familiar with the nuances.**

   To encourage the development and emergence of existential intelligence, we must be acquainted with the most widespread religious and philosophical systems. Seek the company of like-minded people and discuss with them the progress humans have made in this respect.

2. Open up.

Develop the capability and inclination to get closer to the great questions of life - life, death, values, truth, happiness, etc. How do you formulate the questions correctly and how do you answer them? Train yourself.

3. Mix up the abstract with the material.

The most important practical application you must be aware of is that your position is determined by your own decision making and attitude. Our system of values will vary depending on the decisions we make and how they affect our human relations. This also applies to business relationships. For example, a company undertaking social responsibility and social sensitivity training is highly dependent on the leader's existential intelligence.

Even Howard Gardner did not accept existential intelligence officially as a ninth intelligence type. Still, I thought it would be interesting to give some thought to this talent, ability, lifestyle... whatever we call it. Some people are indeed spiritual and sensitive to humanity's great questions. It is positioned in the center of their lives.

So why not consider bringing out the most of it?

Chapter 13: How to discover your strengths?

What do you want to be when you grow up?

People frequently ask children this question. I think there is no adult who does not remember their biggest childhood dream: truck driver, firefighter, captain, doctor, polar explorer, lion tamer, actress or actor, officer, or astronaut. It is almost impossible to list all the choices. Remember the beginnings, the first experiences, and the end results. Dig down to the depths of your being and discover yourself again.

What's that burning desire inside you that makes you restless even to think about? What makes your heart pound and opens up your mind and soul?

Let me tell you something: you are unique. You have something that nobody in this world possesses. You can be great in (at least) one thing that you can master, perfect and give to the world.

Do not let anybody discourage you. Don't try to fulfill others' expectations. They don't know your strengths or callings as well as you.

In previous chapters, I described nine types of intelligences: verbal, logical-mathematical, visual-spatial, body-kinesthetic, musical, interpersonal, intrapersonal, naturalistic, and existential. You are gifted with at least one of these. Maybe you are "bilingual" or "trilingual", in other words, you are equally gifted with two or three intelligences. None of them are better than the other; they are different.

So why are they important? You know there's a saying that every journey starts with a single step. But in which direction should you start moving?

The best choice is to find work in accordance with your strengths. Why? Let's picture a fish. What first skill or adjective would we attribute to this animal (and let's not picture a whale)? Good swimmer? Quick? Maybe slim? All these, right? Now let's picture the same fish trying to climb a tree. Now how would we characterize it? Lame, weak, and struggling? It's the very same fish. It matters, my dear reader.

The same rule applies to people. If a person does something that fits him or her, something that gives her passion, something she has a talent in, then that person is happy, inspiring, a "good swimmer." If somebody does something that doesn't give happiness, fulfillment, and that she has no talent for, then she is just like a fish at the base of a tree.

How do you determine your main intelligence type?

Ask questions of yourself. Answer these questions. Practice and start to train your brain. A good question leads to a good answer. More good questions lead to more good answers. A lot of questions and answers can begin to draw out your personality and help you start something.

What's a good question? Why do we care about the answer? Now, that's a very good question! There are two answers to this.

1. **Silver lining.**

   If you're just curious and want to feed your vanity, you answer questions and fill out various tests dishonestly. The answers given to the questions are far from the truth. You polish your ego. But these fake mood-boosters melt away quickly and you stay in the big nothing.

2. **Objectivity.**

   If you want to change your life, then be honest and objective with yourself. Don't do this for the sake of the neighbors; do this for yourself.

Sincerity! Objectivity!

These are two magic words that you should keep in mind! Pay attention to the content and meaning of both, and use your brain to act with these two words in mind so you can find your true strength, your main intelligence. Which is first, second, and third?

Take a piece of paper and pen. It's time to do some work. Only through the written word can we find the true answers. I'll ask four similar questions. Write each down on a separate sheet of paper giving your most honest and accurate answers.

- What did I want to be when I was little?
- What was my dream 5 - 10 - 15 years ago?
- How do I see myself at this moment?
- Who do I want to become in 5 - 10 - 15 years?

To each of the four questions write ten attributes, skills, strength, which define your current state. Write the characteristics from 1 to 10 under each for better transparency. Do not read any further until you're finished. This may take a few minutes, hours, or even days.

The characteristics of your childhood are important because at that time you're building your personality and your dreams into your subconscious. These dreams and desires are stowed and only waiting for an external stimulus to break to the surface once again. There are huge power reserves in those dreams, you just have to find the key to open the door. It is important to be honest in an objective manner.

When this is done, you can move to the next step.

Find the characteristics that can be found on all of the four sheets.

Such repetitions can occur more than once. It is also possible that there is no such quality that appears on all the four sheets, only on three or two.

Now take a clean sheet of paper, and write on it all those characteristics that could be found on all four (or three) sheets. How many of them are present four times? Which are those? This is very important.

Interpret the results. This is another essential step you should not rush through. In the previous chapters (4 to 12) I talked about the basic characteristic of human intelligence types and what criterions describe them. Scroll back and look through the book. In what intelligence type do your common characteristics fall?

The more characteristics that can be associated with an intelligence type, the more accurate the information you possess will be. These indicators of intelligence – from the "I was, I am, and I will be" periods assist in further development. You'll find out:

- What are your general characteristics?
- How were you?
- How are you?
- How do you want to be?
- What are your strengths?
- What are your weaker, just "light" abilities?
- Where do you need improvement?

Do not forget to always keep in your mind: sincerity and objectivity.

John D. Rockefeller, businessman and multi-millionaire, once said, "I pay more for the ability to get along with people, than any other skill." Why is this important? It's because the vast majority of people are looking for job security. There are far fewer people creating jobs.

The biggest US companies recruit employees mainly based on their personality. The diplomas and expertise are not as important as possessing the right personality traits. If the candidate has a good character, then he/she can be taught to do the required tasks successfully. You can have five degrees, four doctorates, and know almost everything, but if your personality is ugly, no one will want to spend the time, money, and energy to change it.

85 percent of what we achieve in life depends on how we get along with others.

85 percent of our happiness comes from finding the right partner.

Honestly and objectively assess your current state.
Where are you now?
Write down what you want to achieve. Life starts now!

What happens from this moment on is up to you.

Chapter 14: What's your main intelligence type? How can you make a living from it?

What is your main intelligence type? What activity makes you the happiest? What do you love doing? If the answer to these questions does not pop into your mind instantly maybe you should flip the coin to the negative. In other words, what do you hate doing? What activities leave a bitter taste in your mouth?

For example, you hate numbers but work as an accountant. This is quite tragic. Or you hate music, and you're a doorman at a music academy where music comes from ten different doors.

Sometimes it is helpful if you exclude some intelligence types and consider only those that aren't awful for you to begin.

Another good approach is to think back to what

questions you asked your family when you were little. Like, "I'd like to play guitar," or "I'd like to take a long walk in the forest." The activities you want to do reflect a desire to subconsciously improve your main intelligence type. Whatever you request most can lead you to your main intelligence type.

A third way to find your main intelligence type is to think about how you treat your spouse, friends, or children. If your main type is interpersonal intelligence, you often take your significant others to social events and organize big parties for your loved ones. If you're gifted with intrapersonal intelligence, you'll buy some self-development books or a ticket to a self-improvement course as a gift for your friends and family. Ask yourself how do you most often express your appreciation?

Remember, this is a way of uncovering your main intelligence type but not a rock-solid indicator. Gifting habits can be learned from your parents. If your dad often gave psychological books to your mom, or flowers, you may do the same as an adult. It doesn't necessarily mean your strength is intrapersonal or naturalistic intelligence. Still if other behaviors agree, observing how you treat others can be a confirmation of your main intelligence type.

Let's say now, for argument's sake, that you know your primary intelligence type. Now you know you love doing this and you're good at it, but the next question is how can I make a living from it?

This is a question I have been thinking a lot about. And once I came across Cal Newton's book, *So Good They Can't Ignore You*. The main message of this book might seem counterintuitive at first. The writer says you should not pursue your passion; it is the fool's method. What you should do is be ok with grinding a little bit, and when you grind in whatever industry you collect something called "career capital." When you have enough career capital, you can exchange it for whatever makes you satisfied in life. This, in some degree, can be creativity, freedom in your occupation, and a bigger impact. The basic message is that it is not the industry or the actual job itself that matters, but the freedom and approach you take with it.

What do you think about this my dear reader? To some extent I agree with Mr. Newport. Indeed, there is no point in being reckless. If you have no savings, nothing to buy bread, and your dream doesn't become profitable, it will poison the entire process. A Spanish proverb: where hunger knocks on the door, love jumps out on the window.

Let's think this through with my favorite theory, Maslow's hierarchy (or pyramid) of needs. The theory states that human needs can be divided into five main categories. You can not move up until the lower level is fulfilled.

1. The lowest level consists of basic needs like eating, sleeping, and meeting basic physiological needs. If somebody is hungry they're not so open to listening to speeches

about self-realization and living a better life. That person will say, "ok, ok just give me some food." It makes sense. Until the very basic needs are met, you won't be able to focus on anything else. So in order to step to the next level you need to make sure you're ok at this level. One of my favorite motivational speakers, Peter Szabo, shared an example in one of his presentations. He was often asked to give motivational speeches to homeless people to encourage them to seek a better life. His answer was this: "I don't think this is a good idea. Not because I don't care about them or think their life cannot be better, but because at the level they are, they won't be interested."

2. The second level is safety. If the first level's needs are met, a person can start to care about their personal, financial, and health safety. This means that in order to move to level three you have to be ok with your

health and economic condition as well as your family and property's safety. Many people with potential get stuck at this level.

I don't like to demonize things, but I think television is to blame for this matter. Please don't get me wrong, I don't want to discourage anybody from reading or listening to the news, but think about how it makes you feel. This person died, that exploded, terrorists attacked... It is full of negative vibes, fear, and tragedies. If I listen to the news, by the end I feel anxious, like my safety is threatened. I don't feel safe anymore, so I lose control over the higher levels of this pyramid. And this happens to so many people. The one thing they are not conscious of is that they cannot change the news. They can't influence it so why worry? Why not climb higher on the personal development ladder instead of getting stuck in a state of anxiousness? If you read the news, I strongly recommend letting it go afterward, unless you're the president of the United States. Then you can have an influence.

3. The third level is the level of love and belonging. Family, romantic relationship, and friends are on this level. Here is another example of where personal well-being prevails. If you are not ok with your own physiological needs and safety, you cannot focus properly on others. It is important for people to feel that they are needed. Every man wants to be treated as an individual and to take responsibility. If you feel needed and appreciated, you'll have a sense of importance.

4. The level of esteem. Here people are ok with physiological needs, they feel safe and loved so they have a real chance to improve themselves without any distractions or negative feelings. Self-confidence, self-respect, and respect of

others' achievements can reach great levels if you focus on them.

5. The highest level is self-actualization. This is the level where dreams come true. Unleashed creativity, morality, high-level problem solving, and lack of prejudice all belong at this level. Living your main intelligence type is on the highest level here.

There are a few lucky people who can live by their strongest intelligence from the second level -- the first level has nothing to do with it. That's the level of basic instincts.

Those who are doing something that is not their passion shouldn't hand in their resignation tomorrow. They won't be happy painting all day if they are kicked out of their apartment. Here's my suggestion:

- First things first, accept your situation

as it is for now. Unless you have a better option, do not do anything hasty. If you cannot change your position right now, change something you can: your thoughts about it. Stop looking at it as a burden, but the necessary evil you need to move through until you have the career capital you need. In order to focus on the fifth level of the pyramid, you shouldn't crush level two.

- Introduce it slowly into your life: whatever your passion and talent is, you should have it in your life even if you work in a different field. Some people can be fully content keeping their passion as a life-long hobby. Those hours spent with their favorite pastime can invigorate them so much they don't care about the minor nuisances anymore. Are you crazy about sports? Do something every day after work. Practice and learn actively, and if you feel your hobby is ready to be taken to the next level, take the necessary steps. Only then.

- The edge of glory: if you are ready to make a living from your passion, but something is keeping you back, analyze the reasons why. Determine if your fear of failure is justified. For example, if you've become an excellent painter of amoebas, but are hesitant to open an amoeba art gallery, maybe you're right. Maybe this isn't a good idea. But if you are 100 percent positive your passion is something that others could profit from also, maybe the "problem" is at level four of the pyramid. Maybe you need more self-confidence. I think the difference between doing an activity as a hobby and a career is how useful it is to others – thus how marketable. I know it sounds a bit materialistic, but if you sell something people want nobody will question whether or not you deserve the money. Brian Tracy is a millionaire; he did what he wanted most of his life, but I don't envy him any of his pennies. He worked hard and helped thousands or maybe millions of people with his thoughts and courses. Wealth is a direct consequence of a well-executed skill.

- Don't forget how easy it is to fall back. Reaching level five on the pyramid doesn't guarantee you'll stay there. Continuous work must be done in all the previous levels to maintain this high-level position. Let me share an example, please don't be offended. Let's say you're on top of the tops, the world's greatest CEO; however, if you need to pee you fall right back to level one in a second. The greater this urge grows the less you'll be able to concentrate on anything other than a proper British "water cooler" or, at least a bush. This rule applies to higher levels too. If your daughter was in a city just hit by an earthquake, you'll be crazy-terrified until you get news she's ok. The point here is to know that continuous work must be done on all levels to stay at level five. It's impossible to stay there 24/7. The most you can do is to quickly overcome any issues that drag you to lower levels.

If you plan on changing your lifestyle, first do some research to learn what is needed to be able to monetize this passion. Some people, because they are so focused on their passion, don't think about what they need to be good at it. I can't tell you what exactly is needed because every profession requires different research. Collectively I can tell you two things: be true to your passion, and dig deep to discover how you can combine it with your market's demands.

Chapter 15: Focus Like an Eagle

People today experience many distractions – everything is more diverse now.

For example, when it comes to something as simple as cereal, you have many options. When it comes to hobbies, you have even more diversity. I don't know how much time you spend thinking through your choices in a grocery store, my dear reader, but I spend a lot. Sometimes I contemplate about price, value, and other times I don't care about the price and prefer to focus on the quality or flavor. Finally, I choose something, but I wasted so much time that I don't feel good about my choice.

If such everyday nonsense like grocery shopping distracts people, imagine how much distraction is caused by the activities that concern the improvement of your abilities and specific intelligence.

Let's say you want to learn to play an instrument flawlessly. Which instrument? Where? What is the cheapest means of learning? Who is the best instructor? What is the best brand of that instrument? When will you have time? Shall I go on?

You will have so many questions in your head that you'll just sit in front of the television making up excuses why not to do it. You'll never have a hobby, not to mention a skill advanced to the level of perfection that can provide you a new source of income or joy. It's too easy to get lost in the ocean of options and questions. This is called analysis paralysis.

So how can you simplify the process of choice? How can you find the best solution with minimal time investment?

1. **Decide what you want to do.**

By now you should know more or less what your intelligence type is, or at least which you want to improve.

Let's say you want to improve your body-movement intelligence. What do you like regarding motion? Do you like team sports or are you a lone ranger? You might hate running, but do you like water? If you already tried out many sports, think back which did you like the most. If the answer is none, then body-movement intelligence may not be your thing at all.

What really matters is to have a clear vision of what you want to do. Write down on paper three columns: love, hate, never tried. Then take your time to think about as many aspects as possible regarding sports. Let me give an example.

Love: balls, running, cardio exercises, be indoors, high performance.

Hate: team sports, too much crowd, doing sport outdoors.

Never tried: competitive sports, accuracy-focused sports.

Let's pretend that this is your list. In this case maybe, you should try table tennis. It is a ball involved, you can play alone, it is played indoors, and involves a surprising amount of high-performance cardio. You know how I found it? I searched online. Tennis as an option, too, but tennis is mostly outdoors, with the possibility of many spectators.

This is the very first step you should make. Write your love-hate list as long to try to reduce your options down to one. (Maybe two – just in case you hate the first choice or it does not comply with the next points.)

2. Set your priorities.

What is the most important aspect of the self-development activity you are looking for? Do you have a low budget and want something cheap? Do you have a tight schedule and want something easily accessible? Are you a high performer and want to learn from the best?

Take a paper and pen and write them down with bullet points. This is my top priority; this is second...

Let's stick to table tennis. If you have money, but you just a small amount of time you could buy your own table tennis equipment if you have the place at home, and hire a private instructor who comes to you on schedule. If you have time, but no money, there are cheap gyms where you can practice with other people in similar shoes.

If you have neither time nor money – but you'd really like to play, you need to get creative. Try to collect some colleagues to persuade your company to invest in cheaper table tennis equipment for Christmas as a common gift for workers. This way you can access your game before or after work and most probably there will always be someone around who would like to play.

Whatever the case, there are always ways to make your choice of activity fit your priorities.

3. **Decide why you want to do it.**

You should also decide what your level of engagement in this new activity will be. Would you like to do it as just a hobby, or are you willing to invest more time in it as a lifestyle choice? You must know that these levels require a different amount of time, money, and dedication as an investment.

It can be quite easily decided based on your priorities in point 2. So if you want to be a professional table tennis player, but you don't have the time and money for it, you must pay a high price if you still want to go for it. Would you pay it?

Likewise, if you have the time and money, but you only want to do it as a hobby, do not invest more in it than it is proportional with your goals. If you want to keep the benefits in balance with the investment to make the most from your money and time, you shouldn't overdo it. What I mean here is that you don't need professional equipment or two hours of mental preparation for each match.

4.   **Revise your priorities. (Something for something.)**

Do this step a day after you wrote your priorities out in the prior steps. Now that you have slept a night on your great idea of starting a new self-development activity, make sure this is really what you want and how you want it.

Be realistic with your plans. If you are 45-years old, you probably won't make it to the Olympic table tennis team anymore, but you still can be the guru of your company, your neighborhood, or your family.

5. **Avoid distractions.**

It doesn't matter if you play table tennis as a hobby or take it seriously; respect your time with that activity. You do it for yourself. You carefully chose this among many, many other things you could have done. You invested time in making the choice, so make it count.

Put your phone on silent mode and try to empty your brain of external distractions and stressors. Those hours you spend with your chosen self-development activity should be only about yourself.

6. Don't forget what the main point of the activity is.

Focus and learn. Do not forget that at the end of the day, this new pastime you have is for your development and improvement. It serves the purpose to make you better in something you were born to do. Whatever reasons may lie behind this activity choice of yours, the main purpose is to make you better than you were a day before. It doesn't matter if it is table tennis, a communication course, a philosophy book, or jogging every morning – you have to give 100% focus and dedication to it.

100% commitment can make the difference. It surely makes the difference if you make this activity for a living. But it also can give you a lot if you simply do it to escape your daily rat race.

Follow these six steps, be super focused, and choose the best activity to maximize your greatest strength.

Chapter 16: How do you change your "dark side?"

I cannot emphasize enough the importance of self-love. If you don't love yourself, you can't make others happy either. Some people can go to extremes hating themselves. Is it possible to love somebody you hate?

This is a difficult question to answer. Hate is provoked by unhappiness, dissatisfaction, and anger. If you live a life you hate, it becomes a burden to go on with it day after day. People often make promises to themselves that they will not keep. "Just resist a few more weeks, months, years… " you tell yourself. "You can't change now; your mortgage must be paid. But when that's done then…"

In the meantime, you know that nothing's going to change. You feel helpless and that creates rage against the world, the system, and everything but yourself. Thus you lose your sense of responsibility. If you don't take responsibility you lose control of your actions. You'll feel even more exposed to circumstance. This enhances your rage and bitterness against the world... Should I go on?

It is a vicious cycle and you will fall deeper and deeper into hating life. Hating your life and hating yourself go hand in hand. Bad circumstances and unhappiness can make you feel depressed and powerless. You might feel you'll never get through this. But then, what's the point of living?

Even if somebody is successful and rich... and hates what they do, they may have the same thoughts. *I hate my life. There's no purpose in what I do. I don't even have the time to spend the money I've earned. What's the point?*

These are not my thoughts dear reader; these are the thoughts of many unhappy people around the world.

Where's the way out? How can you find what you love and do it without it leaving a bitter taste in your mouth?

The answer is simple. Everything you do, do it with 100 percent dedication! Give it your best shot; you got this!

Why should you do it? Because there is nobody in the world more important than you. I know it sounds selfish, it may be weird to accept this the first time you hear it, and it is natural to think you love your spouse or children more than yourself that you'd give your life for them, but think about it. How could you give something that you don't possess?

It's like when the flight attendant demonstrates the safety regulations. What do they say? Put your life jacket on first; only then can you help others. You cannot help anybody until you are out of danger. The same rule applies to love and self-love.

It all begins with a decision. You decide that from this moment you will change your life. So far, the events and the impact of the environment influenced your everyday life. From now on you will be the captain. It is simple – but not easy.

Get off the couch and turn off the TV. You must stop dulling yourself and whine no more about your current situation. Remember, everything that has happened to you today, in this moment, is the result of your previous decisions and THOUGHTS. Just decide:

ENOUGH!

If you focus on the intelligence types, the development of interpersonal and intrapersonal intelligence can be especially helpful in keeping you on track with your decisions.

Intelligence can be interpreted as a method of action. Intelligence does not depend on your university degrees, or your family background or connections. Your intelligence is a result of a way of thinking and action-oriented approach. The previous chapters talk about this in details.

- What do you like to do?
- What can you do right now?
- What do you need?

These are basic questions that you should be able to answer right now. These answers are most similar in your optimal intelligence. When you answer only two questions similarly, you face a situation that requires attention.

Think about it, plan it, and do it! Here and now! Identify what your passion, your needs, and your potential. Tell yourself: I CAN DO IT NOW!

Now do it. The greatest disappointment you can feel is when you lose credibility in your own eyes. When a promise is made but isn't kept, it creates a sense of emptiness, a sense of unfinished business. And the worst case is when you don't keep a promise you made for yourself.

And the negative spiral may start up again. It is important to stay credible in your own eyes. Better start with smaller promises. *Today I will walk home instead of taking the bus.* Or, *this weekend I'll have a picnic instead of watching TV.* Then work up to the bigger ones like, *I'm going to learn to play the violin.*

Remember to build up credibility, take responsibility, and keep promises to yourself. You are number one. Learn to accept the person you are now. Stop saying, "I'm still bad at something, but..." Forget this. You are good as you are now. Of course, you can and should improve if you want, but you need to be able to accept yourself as you are now. If you accept yourself, you'll be able to love yourself. If you love yourself, you'll love your innate abilities and intelligences. If you love them, you'll love using them. If you love using them, doors will open where you previously only saw walls. You'll be unstoppable!

Chapter 17: Happiness is a decision

If you don't want to be an unhappy person then stop being an unhappy person. The only person who has control over your mind is... you. Happiness is mostly a decision. Of course some events may influence it but at the end of the day you have the choice to focus on the happy events.

If you feel unhappy, search for the cause and change it. In my opinion bad habits are the main reasons for discontent. The bad habits put you in this unhappy position. You have to replace them with good habits. Conformity, laziness, greed, fear, procrastination - and I could go on with this list (hours spent in front of the television, talking nonsense with your buddies, or just aimlessly daydreaming) - are the results of long-standing habits. Leaving these habits behind takes time.

First, we must learn new things. We cannot make ends meet relying only on our experience. That is an outdated concept. Be opened to new things. Be persistent and do not give up. Vow to yourself that you will not give up until you achieve your goal, you passion, what you were born to do!

The length or difficulty of the road ahead can make a lot of people stop before they even cross the start line. Set off and take the first step. Divide the distance into manageable stages. Do a little bit more than you're comfortable with. Undertake a little bit more and keep your commitments. Only in this way is it possible to begin to develop a new habit that will make you stronger. Believe in yourself. Believe that you can do it.

The first time you get paid for doing something you love, you may feel guilty. This is because it is programmed into us that work is the necessary evil that you must do in order to survive. When you begin to make a living from your hobby, people will tell you things like, "you won't be able to make ends meet." They may tell you it is too risky or that you'll regret it. Do not listen to them. If you are true to your heart, you've done all the research you need to start your business with as little risk as possible. Just do it. Just let their remarks go.

This also applies to you. Do not badmouth others. Do not judge others until you have the necessary information. Ask yourself the question – *If I was in his place...?* Why should you ask such a question? Because you are also bothered when others judge you without knowing or thinking about what you are going through. All that matters is what is good for you and not what people are say.

Learn to love. Love the obstacles because, if you can overcome them, they can show what you are capable of. You will be stronger. Love the darkness because you know that it co-exists with the light.

Pay attention to the signals from the environment. Everything around you lives and exists. We're part of a large wholeness. Opportunities are in you; you just have to learn how to take advantage of them. Your talent, skill, and knowledge is worthless if you do not use it.

Every day you want a bit more than the previous day. Every day you do a little bit more than you did the day before.

Trace the path you have chosen. There are so many people who start out the same way and ... stop or give up before the finish line. On bumpy, curvy roads many people lose their faith, their confidence, and their endurance.

YOU WILL GO ON. Maybe you only have to go until the next turn and there, behind the corner success is waiting. It is also possible that you need to turn around several bends before you'll see the finish line, but you will persevere and get through it your way.

Provisions for your journey...

I could summarize again what I already told you, my dear reader. Everything I told you in this book, I meant.

This book was inspired by my own metamorphosis. Everything I shared in this book worked for me. I worked for a good company, for a good salary (relative to my country's average income). Still I felt unhappy, trapped, and absorbed in this thing we call the rat race. I felt that at the age of twenty-five all my life was about bills and getting a better phone, bigger apartment, and cooler clothes.

I worked sometimes thirteen or fourteen hours per day just to collect all the junk I thought I needed to be happy. Of course, when I finally had the money to buy the stupid, expensive thing I wanted, it didn't make me happy. I felt my time was wasted; I didn't add any value to the world or myself. Deep down I knew I wasn't born to be a translator at a multinational company. I hated repeating other people's words that I didn't believe in.

One day I said, "enough is enough!" I turned in my resignation and started doing what I enjoyed -- writing and teaching other people to accept themselves. Right now I feel like I've never been happier, more free, or more satisfied with my life. The transition period wasn't easy. But it was worth it. I will never regret choosing me, accepting who I am now, and who I want to be.

I'll say goodbye with an inspirational quote from Cheryl Strayed. I hope it will help you too.

> "Don't surrender all your joy for an idea you used to have about yourself that isn't true anymore."

I wish you all the luck in the world in finding your passion, exploring your intelligence, and giving value to yourself.

P.S.: If you have some questions please don't hesitate to contact me on zoemckey@gmail.com. I welcome any kind of constructive opinion as well. I'd like to know how can I help better so please share your ideas with me. If you'd like to get helpful tips from me on a weekly basis, visit me at www.zoemckey.com and subscribe. Thank you!

CPSIA information can be obtained
at www.ICGtesting.com
Printed in the USA
LVOW11s1347161116
513225LV00001B/18/P